Manual *for* Living

PITT POETRY SERIES
Ed Ochester, *Editor*

Manual *for* Living

Sharon Dolin

UNIVERSITY OF PITTSBURGH PRESS

Published by the University of Pittsburgh Press, Pittsburgh, Pa., 15260
Copyright © 2016, Sharon Dolin
All rights reserved
Manufactured in the United States of America
Printed on acid-free paper
10 9 8 7 6 5 4 3 2 1

ISBN 13: 978-0-8229-6406-3
ISBN 10: 0-8229-6406-6

for Sam
dove sta memoria

Know first who you are, and then adorn yourself accordingly.

—Epictetus

Contents

II. *Black Paintings*

III. *Of Hours*

Manual *for* Living

Just This

Not the patter of collide
not the click of revive
not the curls of worry
not the tail of sorry

not the kiss of clever
not the mint of comply
not the needle of haste
not the fear of dare

not the fences of morn
not the omen of bowmen
not the harrow of alarm
not the praise of arms

not the warp of lean
not the downpour of mean
not the brawn of prowl
but the flame of now

not the lash of forever
not the dirge of deny
not the wristwatch of chaste
not the cuticle of rare

not the nethers of scorn
not the barrow of shadow
not the widow of gaze
but the arms of praise

I. Manual for Living

after Epictetus

Approach Life as If It Were a Banquet

Or a lunch basket crammed with
pleasure in restraint and blood oranges.

Your rightful portion averts your ireful potion:
caress what can't be blessed, cup shadows under breasts.

Let pass what's out of ken: lover, job, riches,
a ripe peach
               until it reaches you.

Bring salt for your honey, lime for your grenadine.
Money's not your fault.

You're a feathered peahen
                       preening for marzipan men.

Impeccable models, often peccable,
drop their pants at inopportune
                       instants of impatience.

Implore no more
           for what is, is no more.

Always Act Well the Part That Is Given You

Be it fop or magistrate, Wall Streeter or window
    cleaner, stalker or star flower: inhabit it with gusto—
      though knowing it's a role,

an art, may make you cynical or quizzical.
    If you're unsure about your part?
      Become a stand-in; as understudy,

you yet may pace the boards. If uncertainty is laced
    into the act—as though as street cat you had
      to figure whether to leap that ledge

or stay—make uncertainty your role: the half-slipped
    mask, hesitant dancer, jittery lover. Rehearse
      reluctance with vehemence. The wavering scene

unwaveringly.

Briefly Accept Events as They Occur

Eventually, you have to rail, don't you,
    every time it doesn't go your way.
        Erase the world? Ever the charmer
    the world will win. Even the flayer
knows when to accede defeat. Eventually.

Who hasn't awakened to the ecliptic shock
    of everything failing?
        Where you err is in thinking you control
    what befalls or eludes you and when.
Early storms are the rule (until this year).

Even the vulture picking at your liver
doesn't always wait till it regenerates.

Care for What You Happen to Have—There Is Nothing to Lose

So what if your beloved has died
    or moved away, your possessions
    repossessed for what you cannot pay.

As long as your breath's chest falls
    then rises: Go. Water the ferns
    of the brood you're in. Groom your fussy

griffon. Smooth your rugose skin.
    Voyage to that Dead Sea inn
    where all your past lovers exfoliate

and float away. What you have is what you seek—
    what you failed to find, let be
    another's gold mire.

Observe the blue dragon
    may be purple-winged. And that peach pie
    you've been saving for guests?

Stick two forks in. Now go call your son.

Desire Demands Its Own Attachment

Daunted by disastrous consequences?
Don't be. Everyone—even you—
delights in devil-scape. Do you
rue more than revel?

Disappointed more than
detached? Even the dog
detours from the stick.
Rein in desire. (Rainin'

Death's ire.) A porous heart of tears
decked out as diamonds (poor us).
If someone's declining from their
window as you below go by,

if all they fling is damage,
depart, deafened to desire—
that demon, dire.

Everything Has Two Handles

Whether to grapple the hurt or hold
the calm: can reason spread
where ire infests the mind?

The handle you refuse
to grasp proclaims you more than one
you lurch to reach.

Why mire in the right/wrong amphora song.

No vigilance in this choir of one.
No fast hook in the urn's
broken-off arm.

Vie with hot verities.

The pie is getting cold.

Faithful Is Not Blind Belief

It's hateful to be mistaken or forsaken.
Worse yet to be bitter, full of spite.
Which is why you should believe
all is not random:
                        That fretful

marriage that fled you led you
to your teenage son, that job you didn't get
to this mid-morning bliss.
                        Divine plan?

Tell that to the beggar by your subway stop
with rags for shoes. But hey, didn't he choose
to spiral down to drink the brown?
                        And you—

so easy to reject such views while ordering
your daily frappe. Is God then for the middle class?

A certain kind of faith in providence, perhaps. So
grasp your cuppa and let it lift you up.
                        Chin-chin.

Everything Happens for a Good Reason

Good. Comedy may equal tragedy
plus time—as good reasons may
be gall gilded over trust.

Great that he gamed you. Grand
she's gone gloomy, gorged on hemlock.
Colossal you've got no gig, no guy, no granita.

Greet each gravity with gratitude like a cavity.

If every dark cloud has a gelato-
swirl lining, why are you groveling there
all gemütlich, shivering under someone's

malicious downpour, still
goo-gooing up?

Happiness Can Only Be Found Within

Which is why you mustn't bore more nor
    adore easily. Contract
    within. *Denser*

means more than *hard to get.* Do not
    be buffeted about by outward
    gaze or fashion. Whatever

nameless muse—whatever flair for news—
    woos you, it behooves you
    to become the *you*

you are. That platinum screen babe? Miss
    kinky-haired obscene? Or that
    young libertine?

How do you know each doesn't churn alone
    inside her head in paisleyed
    autumnal bed

while you stay up composing blues
    on the Aeolian harp of you? No matter
    you roam the Côtes du Rhône,

dwell in penthouse, farmhouse of stone,
    or a single peeling room:
    it's you who gets

to choose to scat the blues. Forget about
recognition by your fickle peers.
All honor, steady bliss

comes from the peerless pear you raise
to your own lips.

No One Can Hurt You

Hurt havens in the mind.
Have you been harrowed by havoc?
Hackles up? Hazarded by hearsay?

Pull back. Reverse binoculars:
See your interior life as landscape.
Huddle and don't breathe.

Hustle and sigh.
Hug yourself continually.

Make Full Use of What Happens to You

In the face of broken
    build a tower of breath
In the eye of deceit
    carve a hive of light
In the rumble of regret
    fashion a new net
In the oracular gut
    leaven what's left
In the fall of grief, harvest
    winter wheat
In the infested wound, bring leeches
    to swoon
In the empty bed, writhe
    a pelvic bone
In the stung heart, harrow
    a new song
In Fortuna's backswing
    let fallow fill wings

Events Themselves Are Impersonal and Indifferent

What? You mean that steel step
        didn't mean to gash your toe? Nothing personal,
        your lover didn't care
that you became a basket of frozen grapes

wintered on the isle of his
                        no-more-longing-for?

That the one whose jackaled heart
        burst on the bedroom floor:
        his death impersonal—indifferent—jinxed by chance?

Be a sleuth. Find the hidden opportunity
                        in misfortune's juba dance?

Plucked tail from the untwitching
        maggoty beast. Jangled grace in a man
        leveled by cancer-eating blood—
or bone—or her viral load.

Oh, forgive yourself for not jubilating in the shadows
        of this bosky perch, where light echoes off
        leaves the way words echo off your jaundiced heart.

Some gift. Yes, the impersonal thrift.

Know What You Can Control and What You Can't

Undress your wish to direct your nevertheless.
   Your chant of self-promo—just cant,
      your face—a faltering race

away from that withered fate.
   What others think is a sink-
      hole of jitters that drinks you

to fretting—and you'll miss the dance.
   So what if you live in a mosh pit of who
      did what to whom and what you blat

about someone will be blared about you. Why not
   abide inside the flicker of mind, a companionable
      controlled clime (your own thermostat, preset).

Power is such a fickle hour, mean wealth
   shackled to itself. Only by
      attending to what is outside

your purview (repute is a beaut)
   will you be undone. And that's no fun.

Living Wisdom Is More Important Than Knowing About It

So don those russet/saffron robes,
but does that make you wise?

In color, perhaps,

                    but in choler . . .

perhaps not.

Our Duties Are in Relation to One Another

Feel unique in roiling solitude? Oh, you are not alone
though you may feel fallen, snow up your nose. Join
    with others in your dank reclusion.

How do you find something worth saying?
How do you find desire to find desire
    to find something worth saying?

And yes. That is where you might be: twice—
or is it thrice—removed in a receding
    mirror of acedia. Finding a way to

find a way to want to find a way back in
to conversation. This is what negative numbers
    (a negative soul) feel like: You want to want to want . . .

If you go back far enough—lateral excavation—
will you hit bone? So many converging lines yakking
    to themselves over a haywire switchboard

you used to find out who you were through
cookie crumbs tossed down your own path.
    Now that you have no crumbs, don't

even have pockets to turn out—only the memory
of such acts, such things: How weary, stale, and
    profligate it seems to be to plasticize these

lines. You're in a hamless state of mind.
Now get out and talk to anyone your age: like you
        they've all got Death studded on the tongue, which

livelies up the talk they walk.

Pay No Attention to Things That Don't Concern You

Such as dazzle-tales of what others
pin upon you—or disdain.
By staying out of the rain

of public downpour, drinking in
the fumes of *Me-Me-Me*
jockeying to be: riding

a fast horse out of control into broken.
Respect the force between your legs
that carries you at whatever pace

into forward. You'll end the same:
by fire, water, cerebral bleed, crash, or slurring
pain. Along the way stay single-minded.

Give up on self-belief
you've got to seek
in crow's feet

of another's smile.

All Advantages Have a Price

As all vantages, iced with nice, are noosed.
Born—or slept—into or killed for:
      A stolen fame is

twice reclaimed. So what if twin-forked
delusion floods your veins since birth.
      So what if privilege is a ledge

from which you've never jumped. The teeming source
of the mind bucking its stall no one can ride
      but you. Every spider spinnerets its own

fib. Every liar sups his own bile. And you,
Miss Curds and Whey, since when did your
      glabrous eye, unbotoxed lips not

smirk up party beaus. If you lack her ribbons, her
acclaiming mane, just think how craven,
      she's forsaken labial pairs

for the mohair lap of men. We all wear
hair shirts of our own devise. Choose yours
      with forethought and abandon.

Never Regret

Disavow any backward-glance romance.

To make a picture of where you aren't going.
To make a seizure of where you could've been: You can—
and have—
              spent your life entire wanting

to ruminate the course you might have traversed,
your tongue might have grazed
had you not thrown two teas(e)poons away.
                              (Recall *remorse*

as in *rechewed*.) All the while the silver you've borne:
gaunt heart who stole away his shadow so you
                              lucubrate in pieces.

Fractious boy, tangerine hall of halloo, teal seabed of buoyed-up sex

lose luster as you sink face down
in the muck of spat-up bland
                              under suburban porch lights:

Ye Olde Village Prickly of Regurgitated Regret.

Recognize Mere Appearances for What They Are

Who you are is by no means
                how you appear. If your mate

throws you, raise a shrug
                of conjecture over

what you dread to flee.
                A cloaked face runs

a crooked race. If it's out of your
                control, cave in

to chance. Dismayed by chicanery
                as far away as Golden Bay?

Paddle away from rough surf
                of desire—all jealous wiles.

And you're freed from the chimera of the couple.

Refrain From Defending Your Own Reputation

Who rapped on your
        rep   rapt
ones know that's a snow
        job you can do better
bluster.

Defend yourself?
                Diss back?
        Fend off
              the cape-swirl of
this bull's
        approaching horns

and let him glance you with his
        charge. As you, scarcely scratched,
behind your
        flickering
fan gasp:
        Oh, I guess he hasn't heard

the worst about me yet.

Stick with Your Own Business

Advice being the first covert vice . . .
      stick to your give.

(Flick what don't own
                busy with what don't moan.)

Knowing and attending to what actually concerns you . . .

By being twice nice is all yours (a nice trice),
      tend your own—a Day-Glo ecotone.

The less of others
           you get disheveled in—

be it a broken body's busyness (sheer hissiness)—
      the faster you get

back to your bowl of sticky rice.

Don't Demand That Things Happen as You Wish

but wish for them to happen as they do.
    That twisted foot, brain tumor, hit-
        and-run driver, failure of heart,

your dad's—or your—ischemic stroke: wish for it. Or, rather,
    wish for whatever happens to happen and take it
        as it comes. Wish for the thief to get away

in your Mazerati . . . if he does. Wish for you to miss—then catch—
    your lover's lies when he flies. Wish for that moment
        when you tell the doctor: *Stop*

all-antibiotics-stop-all-food-stop-all-oxygen-stop-all-water.
    Yes. Wish for the ocean to rise, over-
        flow the levees, wish for the flood that relieves you—

as it relieved him—of all future wishes . . . if it does. Yes. Wish for that.

Avoid Adapting Other People's Negative Views

To gaze upon the fatal
without commiserating gloom:

What every friend should be—
not one who rends her coat of doom

nor one who lets her ankle rankle
nor her dogged love to the hounds.

Be the cat in catastrophe
who survives eight more dives.

Though in the clutch of damage
a dame must age,

in the crazy quilt of guilt
it was never your fault.

In the company of morose
always pull out the rose.

Your Will Is Always

yours—no matter you can't amble
    much or gamble, your temples
are wailing like a trombone

or that you've hit a dead-end occupation:
    talker amid texters, reader among scanners,
writer among crosshatchers. Soldier on.

    Though you cower in a trench of how
though you swivet with the fret of why

though your spine has hoisted up
    its white sky flag,
clamber on.

II. Black Paintings

I see only forms that are lit up and forms that are not.
There is only light and shadow.

—Francisco de Goya

Pilgrimage

Do they think they know
　　where they are going—
　　clustered mouth-hives

guitar-strummed
droning in the dusk wind

at the backs of the Madrileños
　　　　　　　　who stretch into a Dance of Death?

Cover their heads,
the bell has already rung.

No one to hear the gasp of vespers

march toward a storm-sky of judgment
　　　　　　　　　　that won't relent.

And I am on the side blatting along
though it is not my journey,

not my song.

The Coven

Conjure me up—goat-bearded, horned—you
    robed silhouette. Conjure me up
out of carbon dirt in a habit

of white, all feet and hands stuck
    on a hunch-
backed stump. Stir, stir for the clapping hiss

your brood of brujas scheme: so kerchiefed
    in fright we cast a spell
so sticky-webbed we've conjured up even you.

And don't think I haven't noticed *you*, sweet ingénue,
    sitting on the side in novitiate black,
hands hidden in a fur muff, unable to clap or snap.

You'll become like me: shriveled crab apple
    they toss to the horses as cante jondo
is squeezed from the throat of a ravening guitar.

Frail Pair

Rest upon it—cane despised
scythe. Not blessed
upon   bat-faced smother-mouths
your back.   Purse open your purse (you're a spent purse)
long beard of last words
        (cane-gripped)
your whole life declining
       into this
   hiss:
      body
        grotto-dark.

Or, Judith

Could be his hand under
    her skirts. Or his blurry
    shoulder on top of which
        crow-black night.

Once you are dead you become nobody—
    or only body—*corps exquis* without
    the head. Light picks out underside of
        her breast-colored elbow

of her raised right arm—her striking arm—
    her left breast left shoulder up to the death mask
    that has become her face:
        Fire-lit. Or blood-lit.

Her bonnet her loose-fallen scorpion ringlets.
    The sword. Perhaps she has not yet done it.
    No blood no blood. Or only a little on
        her lion's paw hand.

Who am I? Her nurse profiled by fire,
    having witnessed—or about to
    witness—my hands filling up
        with prayer or a spell.

After which I'll come running:
        Damp cloths. Water basin.

Saturn

I: Chronos

Time eats me:
    my hands my head
    up to my torso

    my woman's buttocks
      (final pillows
        to rest upon)

    only in shadows
      can I hope to survive
      under printer's ink

    under raven sky
such ravening.

II: Father

Is this what wedlock can come to?
            How could you think
                    you could grip my spine like a
            walnut and prize it open for
the twin halves of flesh.

                        So this the cost of your lap:
                your bearded age, gape-mouthed furor
my skin might hold. Shadows
                you've never tasted: What figure is it whose
                    head grows back? That's me:

de Milo Gorgon in search of herself.
            Your bony knees, stringy thighs
                    may be a Titan's: How could you hope
            to eat my heart (sealed in a canopic jar)
when I'm finally done with you.

III: Resurrected Heart

Replant in a chest of honey
    restart the pump for eyes
        (not devouring coins of . . .)

      river of liquid irises
    slip me in and out

    return me to slaking sheets
the thirsty page.

IV: Natal Chart

Saturn, ringed vapor-slow,
     you always occupy
my first house

settle on my chest,
     you suck air of
ambition from me

[Astrologer's caution:
     Befriend Time. Work
          on long-term projects.]

yet my leonine nature
     is restive, lightning-
          quick for the kill: won't

pause for the fall of
minutes that measure
the distance I have yet to cover.

[*I want to get married*
     in a little
          leopard dress.]

Maja

Mantilla'd in black lace, of course
        I could be Melancholy: foreseeing
      the old man's death and my own penury—
          left with a few coins, some furniture,
his portrait of me as a milkmaid in Bordeaux.
      Even I don't know if Rosario

(La Mariquita as he calls her)
        is his daughter, but she draws
      just like him. If you find me here
        in funereal dress, leaning my elbow
on the tomb he prepared for himself, you'll know
      my razor tongue—unable to pierce

his deaf ears—now cuts
            only itself.

The Fountain

Not in a *muchedumbre* of white
Not with mantillas of black lace
Not as a crone nor as an inquisitor
Nor with a carriage of fire
Nor with petitions nor looking for
Miraculous cures from the waters
Just to bathe my face and hands and feet
Just to scrub off
These persistent worries that gnaw me
Like any stray dog
Any broken guitar

The Reading

So what if I was added in later
    looking up reading the mist of whatever
    bearded mystery lies above.

I'm still listening for the words
    dropped like a sandal off the reader's foot.
    Do you think it's been easy?

Those three have been arguing
    for centuries over
    just what that dab of white

does to the news of us.
    So what if I used to have wings or horns.
    And don't even bother asking about

the one in the back—that
    skeleton who just showed up
    to chide and remind

who cares nothing for words
    nor the fish-scale light
    cast upon them.

Duel with Clubs

Blood streaming tears
　　stream blood down
　　my cheek / ear / neck.

Up to our knees in the sand
　　we're fixed on fighting
　　no matter what stormy nimbus

of sky / dunes / mountains
　　looms around us.
　　Pants cinched with

white ribbon, I may not
　　believe in fate but I do
　　believe in the club / the stick / the thigh

bone of my best steer
　　he tried to steal.
　　If my jacket retains

something of the torero's cut:
　　Let this red make him lower
　　his head and charge.

Two Old Folks Eating

I only believe in darkness
and what light it throws off.

I am neither the bald one
gummy with her glazed look

at what has come for her—
her spoon a spinning top

of destiny—with the face of
someone's forgotten nurse.

Nor the skeletal beggar
who proves there is always one

who is more famished
more flensed of everything

but an attitude of bone.

Atropos or the Three Fates

Black ball of Time from which you spin

    float me on a linen cloud you call my life.

        O you in the back with your mantic
        mirror, how do you know

how long to spill my skein—
black blood of me when I shall

        no longer be? Your sister has
        given us her back, pretends to

            be trimming her own hair.
            Sitting hunched among you,

I know she takes her directive from you,

        Lachesis, looking in your one-way
        glass, reckoning when to trap

            my fleering, my gaze.

The Dog

Nothing. Nobody.
In the eye of the dog
    upward
headed toward what

dark fumbling bumble
    bee light.

Any minute land might smother-wash
        over him
darkness of the returning wave.

Wind might ruffle him
    in the howl-hour of dawn.

Bleary in the dreary
    noon of the deaf man's room.

Dark death of the sun. Black dog.
Yellow black dog. Golden-eared

shadowplay: the color of
    surrender

the shape of
    late hope.

III. Of Hours

Now the hour bows down, it touches me . . .
—Rainer Maria Rilke

Psalm of the Flying Shell (4:30 a.m.)

At what solstice hour do I arise
      (at what daybreak dark do wingtips whir)

knowing I can never see your face

knowing my life is spiraled in the conch
      of consciousness (inside the solar plexus

of space)   how can I see in
      to the wings' filigree I'm fused within?

What does the sea-rushing sound announce
      how decipher the architecture of cells   alchemy

of stars as angels for your will?
      My heart is a volute inside a body-whorled

spire that obelisks
      the air   I am thrumming

your praises as the only way to hear
      with the soul's inner ear

Tell me what you desire of me

Window with Wild Garlic in Wellfleet (5 a.m.)

Cinque-foiled in the wider dark
      of dim-rising day   constant-toiled and
folded inside the winter of stormy say
Instead of sun risen   pale steel dome above
      pond foil-pale   from all windows wood-veined
hope for the miracle of
        burning when Moses's staff struck

Now the heavens' rainstick of jagged
      light and what harbored the menorah
(seven-flamed mirror of our sleeping devout)
now no temple   no priest   only this mouth
        awakened to proclaim

in night's last littoral hour
       O Holy-One-Who-Is-One
in this first day-wave you have
        brushed with such bright foam

How Many Dawns (5:30 a.m.)

chill from your darkling east
    have I dreamt then sensed you
        opening your radiant canopy
            diminishing stars one by one

            hidden in the depths »   then with link upon
        link in the shallows all fish come up
    to feed (I sip my first morning tea)
The awakening gene-chains I first gave

my son » *O happy day*! » to me you gave first
    I think of the cicada's gnawing buzz » my dog's
        first tentative swim » the hazy sun after yesterday's
            rain » your unfailing return amid the city's taxied streets

        and sidewalk splintered light upon myriad faces
      And thee, invisible and necessary as air:
    we breathe you in as do the lilies » the island
rocks » the dog tick on my son's back I flicked

off in a shiver »   all things loved and feared
    There grows the oldest faith all down the chain:
        crow » worm » mussel » mimosa »
            lily of the valley » sea grass » lichen » algae »

All these dawn hours » shade receding to your rising blaze

O your eye blinds   »   your hand
        hovers   »   your heart
    graces   »   your nostrils
flare   »   all living things   tremble   (I bow down)

As hour gives way to hour and night
        yields sway to day   as Tuesday recedes
            to Wednesday and the Sabbath over
                the entire week reigns in candle flame:

            Let the moment »   each unseizable
        instant
    (our indwelling time of you)
    be a sign of your presence ongoing

your everywhere darting »   yet O   so still

Morse and Fractals (Dawn Blessings)

Bless.

In the.

Bless. [*How goodly*]

Yellow. Blessed. [*are*] Lily light.

Egg-white. [*your*] In the. Blessed are. The setting.

You. [*tents*] Moon. Blessed. [*O*] For. [*Jacob. Your*] For night. [*dwelling*]

Sleep. Blessed.

Are.

For. [*places.*]

Removing sleep. [*O*]

From morning lids. Blessed are.

For grief-banishing. For within. Blessed. [*Lord*] For within

Creating hollows [*our God*] holes to live. Blessed. For the first. Are you.

First

piss. For

This. Blessed. [*King*]

For the prayer plant unbending.

[*of the*] For straightening me. Blessed. [*universe*] For

The rooster. Blessed. For distinguishes between. For making me a. [*Blessed*]

Woman. [*who*

has

sanctified] Who

does not wish

to be a man. [*us.*]

For freeing the. Are you. For comforting the.

For healing the. For morning tea. For almond-buttered toast. [*Blessed*] For every

coast

fractaled. Magnified.

[*Blessed are you*]
For apricots. Spreading.   [*for having*]
For my blouse and rants. For my pouts
and pants. Blessed. [*restored*] For glees. (On knees.) [*my soul*]   For breasts and
penises.
For vaginas
and butts.   [*within*
me.]   And inner thighs (and
thoughts). And sighs and frost. For white noise.
For who knows. For clitoral rose. [*Blessed*] Blessed are you. For Mandelbrot
Lightning.
The
Julia Set.
[*are you*]   For
opening the eyes of. For
Serpinsky's Carpet. [*Lord, who*]   For
circulating chi. For lifting [*heals*]   the earth above
the. For rain in pain. Stopped. For [*all flesh*]   all waters of.   Who
directs
the steps
of. For leafy
dragonfish. [*and*]   For healing my
broken. [*performs wonders.*] For griffon-licked. My face. For
to cleave to. My lover. For my son. My sun. [*Blessed. Are*]   For
reached.
My new
each day. [*You.*]
New lay. For letters petaled.

Into.   For song.   [*How goodly*]   For permeates the
world. For scintillas of. Cerulean.   Blessed.   [*are*]   To   [*O Lord.*]   you   [*Blessed.*]   I
bow.

Let Me Thrum (6 a.m.)

a new lay upon this lute for you
Let me hum the new day
of loose strife and lily

Let prayer plant and mallow
let heads and hearts   let heels
and thumbs   feathers and fins
and all things fleet and slug

antennaed and furred
all sing » all shirr » all rub and buzz
and fling their call to you
in song-light as the mist still clings

as the settled dew thins
as all attendant things

in your rising yolk-red grin
unfold and rebegin

With Roses (6:30 a.m.)

I'm empty » quench me with song
I'm guarded » open me as the undine
I'm sleepy » waken me to strum
I'm clipped and shorn of night » with each note brighten me

Let the eight-stringed harp hallow your name
I'm thirsty with praise » let this golden net manna me in your majesty

Leaves of the sycamore wave their shade through my window
         in my underwater sun » they dapple my page
Through me the voice of the sparrow
Through my song the dying heave of the hooked bluefish
         its ribboned gills » the color of bleeding roses
In its last gasps » in the punishing air » so like its birth
         it praises you.

What hook have you placed in my lip?

I seek you in the syllable sighs of the sycamore that sings: *Seek more*
I hear you in the mimosa that murmurs: *My Moses*
I have sought your face in the faces of strangers who jostle me at the market
I have glimpsed you in my son's squint and in my lover's ironic grin
I have sought you in the late-blooming rose of Sharon
I have found you in the spider that makes its web in my kitchen corner
I have seen you in the inchworm caught in its web and in the one scaling my arm

O the world is filled with those who bait the hook and those who are caught
         and you alone know which one we will become
         and when you will catch us up in your celestial net

And all at the moment of birth and at the moment of bloom
      and still all at the scissored instant of death

When the good are trampled upon
      and it is difficult to muster my faith into song

When I waver I pray
      you will set me on the highest rock
For even my doubt is holy and drum-taps your praise

Psalm of Morning Mist

Upon my tongue » pond
(upon gitim » inchworm)
Upon wind chimes » Ruby Meadowhawk
(upon trumpet » fish net)
Upon machalath » mimosa
(upon guitar » sand bar)
Upon bagpipes » red pine
(upon piping plover » banjo)
Upon sitar » sea star
(upon lute » hooks)
Upon flute » float
(woodnote » upon my throat)
Upon oriole » aureole
(upon oud » spruce)
Upon zither » vetiver
(theremin » upon yawn)
Upon neginos » cumulous
(upon gu zheng » black-eyed Susan)
Upon trout » sackbut
(gong » upon bullfrog)
Upon gamelan » quahog
(ukele » upon katydid)
Upon koto » sparrow
(upon stones » bandoneon)
Upon hummingbird » tabor
(kookaburra » upon didjeridoo)
Wind   upon   bullroarer
(green heron » upon steel drum)

Upon mosquito » mandolin

                           (upon slipper shell » cello)

Upon pickerel weed

                 upon Japanese maple (upon » upon)

Upon razor clam » kalimba

                       (upon humpback whale » *Hallel*)

Upon morning dew » kazoo

                        (mouth harp » upon carp)

Holy! Holy! Holy!

                   Praise! Praise!

Thistle and Hull (7 a.m.)

> *My heart is in the East*
> *and I am in the far reaches of the West*
> —Judah Halevi

Now that I greet you after decades of dawn

closed lids   what moon wavers » what
        sun pitches » am I a strawberry to be

dropped from the hull by the hand
        of you?   I lean

toward the East
        where the sun has zenithed

and the bombs still fall

Why must my people remain a thorn
        in the side of the world?

O Lord, your dwelling places are lovely   your presence
        everywhere » even in thunder

that rouses me from my slumber.
        If there were still the Temple

I would bring you a burnt offering
        with the spices you savor

As there exists only what is
        between the temples of each

one of us » let this prayer
          and the scorched hearts of those

in your city   be a meal offering
          I lift up my eyes to the heavens:

My mouth is filled
          with your rainwater song

Spread your peace over us
          Hosannah, O save us

Duet of Tree House and Rain (7:30 a.m.)

Drench me (wood-shingled) »

        I will sing you a downpour

Timber-hewn, I rest upon ruined boughs »

        I am married to the wind

From my half-moon window »

        Give songbirds respite

Nothing brings peace »

        Lure forth prayer-whispers

Like drops falling upon »

        In the bulls-eye of morning

Nor a reminder of the miracle of »

        Flinging myself upon the world

As though inside the tent flaps »

        I enter

      Still a wanderer   »   *Seep in*
I have fenced my heart

        «   Herringboned the sun

Help me raze the pickets

        «   *Recumbent moon*

Zithered in brambles leaves drop

        «   Pond a grey sheet

Their notes upon me

        «   *I keep adding on bars*

Though you put out fires

        «   *There is a shiver at the center*

Of the rainstick world

        «   *Who hasn't begged you for a pause?*

Who hasn't prayed for more?

Rose/Boat (8 a.m.)

What arose
              O heal me
Which boat capsized
                           my faith
                                      O renew it
Upon my ossuary
                     let no one gloat
O heal my friends
                        one whose discs—re-fused—
                                                  suffers a forced recline

the other
with her
collap
sing
accord
ion
spine
                     O please lessen their pain
                                             sub rosa
My bones   are thinning   out
Let me continue to stand   *upright before you*
                                                      as the one late rose
                     withstands
Let my eyes too
                     mottled globes
                                    that float » motes

Never let them blot out

            hummingbird hover

                      mimosa festoons

In the book of you

           let me keep reading

                    In the tangled

        broken-off

            vitreous web   water

spiders   float on   belief   in you

Who lifts up the fallen   Who heals the sick   Who soothes us
hour upon hour   in our ordinary   human unhappiness?

From the canoe   fingers water-trilled   I can almost taste you

Blue Ladder (9 a.m.)

Profusion as a way to
    climb down into the flowers
        Only the tree stands its ground
        in the background »   stones line
    the dreamed-of path
dis/closed to me
    while my eye confuses itself
        with blooming
                This is the third hour of the morning
      where we breathe our way up
    into an apex of light
Blue celestial ladder
    overgrown with plants marks the place
        inside the day where we may enter
        the primordial tree »   sleepy transiting
    between levels
          If Jacob's ladder led to angels going up
and coming down while he slept on a stone
    the missing rungs to this song
        thrust me back into this world
        No one moves between messenger
    and the next prayer
Inside this hour I awaken
    to a wingèd transparency
        struggling up
        inside the tree's bole
    passion leaves bursting through the rungs
And the fruit is always invisible to the root

Blue Window (10 a.m.)

It could be any window
    bricked arch Rapunzeled
        and brisked out to sea
    white caps to capsize
the view of you the sighs of

you capstanning me

It could be any languid blaze
    of distance as the day's page
        turns over its maples
    to the breeze and spartinas
the surface of water gone

spangled white in the ascending
    note of bright   *Shine, shine*
        as I fumble inside
    the origami'd heart of
how to climb out of this sluggard's tower

how to fire up these gifts for you
    when I live in a world that has sped up
        the day   (early morning compressed
    to a lozenge of light)   has even
done away with praise

And I am reeling you in as you are reeling

me in »   without the tug of each
         other how could we exist »   though you did
                  before there was a *me* and do not need me
              except to repair the crack in the shattering
(with prayer)   that took place at the burst

of Creation   So dazzle me lapis
         carnelian »   cobalt »   the richest indigo
                  you can muster   Now pour it down
              on this ten o'clock sea-plunge
where I must dive

to rise to you

Green Laddered Thanksgiving (11 a.m.)

At forest-green   at rungs as trees
        at shore-rim   of shadow-green
(on one high step »   on mixing bowl »   dish towel
            pegged
to archway)   to Japanese maple »   ample
            leaves climbing   I am climbing
            to read   Nature's book in this nook
        in this 21st-century kitchen light »   at chin height
        And all I can do is give thanks   Thanks
for the bullfrog   by my door
    Give thanks   for the cicada's dada
        its persistent *is*   for these limbs   that limn
        that I can still swim   on a whim
        in the green pond   Exceeding thanks   for seeding me
        ceding me Samuel   my son
            whose name means *you heard*
                prophet »   anointer of kings »   rejoicer in all things
                who believes in you
            (*How else could the whole world*
                have been created)
More thanks for   Sono (know who *is*)
    the red griffon   fond I am fond of
    his beard-face »   to look   upon is to laugh
        bark against bark   whose patience
            is devotion »   risks
            drowning »   swimming out »   to me

73

Abundant gratitude   in every latitude   for fashioning me as I am
          a woman (no woe-man   not wombed man)
             morning-slow (mourning, low)   who kneels
                  making patterns   quickening with words
                       (consorts with orts)
                  May all these lines praise you
                       rays   raise you
                       thanks   give
                  for each day's   eleventh hour return
                       (my sojourn)
                  the gathering   bright haze

Lament of Shovel and Bell (Noon)

Closest to sun-strength
at what well do I waver
upon which sky-web do I catch
with which still bell and with what
lavender toll do I shovel
my green self out

                of this daily dolor?

At this noon glower I am sticky with despond
the ensign of my faith a fallen
rainbow caught in the roiling
teal of doubt

             I am praying my brokenness to you

This searing bright has blinded me of your face
See, my eyes are scorched with squinting up
my branches have done flowering
This toil »   however twig-
blunted I offer up

              amidst cloud thunder

O do not abandon me to my enemies now

Urn and Hooks (1 p.m.)

Inside the cerulean-globed hour
        inside suffused buzzings »   pond skimmers »
bullfrog tadpoles resting in sun-shallows

with their fabulous ungainly head-bodies
        and see-through tails   when the eggs
have all hatched

and every living thing feels a columnar surge
        and the dead are eclipsed
by the bright blast of   *Let it crawl*   *Let it sing*

Let it chlorophyll   *Let it feather more*
        mimosa blooms   after last night's full moon
has at last fallen inside the world's urn

now that the sun is at full   blinding bright
        what we squint by   at this robust chickadee
height of hummingbirds dipping

inside pale pink blooms:
        The world's liquid hooks and frond nets
have caught me   Let the robin's song exalt you

and each light-stained leaf recall you and let me
        not forget you   *O Invisible-One-Inside-the-Visible*
not even for an instant

Depth Lure Notebook (2 p.m.)

The Truth must dazzle gradually
—Emily Dickinson

The pond stages a shadow play
        of the dead this afternoon.
Whose lost face do I see
        below the surface blue?

Or is it my own death mask
        I am swimming toward
(that day I pass each year
        my death shroud in wardrobe)?

Or do I see the unborn
        with outsized ears and hair
as wispy as sea grass whose sealed
        lids lure me down

down to the bottom page? O Lord
        do birds have souls?
Is that what made a final squeak
        when my son saw a boy

step on one? Then so must the pine warbler
        stiffened on my doorstep
I flung into the woods. Did they
        both fly up to you »   boundless »

invisible? I want to believe my mother's soul
        has been transformed: Some-
where she lives fifteen and rouged again
        yet hovers still in her former

guise »   the one I knew her in
                the one that loved and raised me.
Haven't I seen the waves of her hair in the wind-
                blown cord grass at low tide »

these six-hour surges when you breathe
                through our liquid world?

Scissored In (3 p.m.)

More fraught than at noon is this
    three o'clock dour when I must scale
        this solitary hover   the unblinking shower
        of thunder   I'm thistled- and
    anemone-stained »   unwrung
by the black dog »   unsown
by the blue hour   My broodings have scissored me in
    to the wave frond of what has or might have been
        Permit me to enter behind the scrim
        inside the emerald grotto and let the fanged cur
    beware of the red griffon (*cave canem* in your
effulgent cave)
who guards this afternoon glower of
    turning back »   of faltering under the currents
        O I am become the windflower anemone undone
        in spring »   left to dissemble in your waning wind-light
I still trust in you   I still believe   you will deliver me
in this temple hour   Split me open
    at the stem   Let these outpourings be
        libations on your cloudy altar
        Let my faith bristle like the thistle   Be me royal-hued
harsh in the desert   I wait for you   in the moody marsh »
the lost woods »   at my lambent desk » my wind's eye
    in the garden   of no turning back
        Please accept this sun-declined song
        I wait for you   I abide in you
O lift me up   *Selah*

Blackberry City and Sundial Talk (4 p.m.): *Time*

takes all but memories in the end
            (in time)   takes even those

            of our tailboned ancestors »   this
the purplest late-fall sun   of my lover's ways (of my own)

of the buildings torn down to make way   of those ghosting my dreams
            of the bridges packed with smeared people walking away

of other bridge walks to hear
            "Crossing Brooklyn Ferry"   the ceremony

            of marriage   even of the brightest
blood birth   at the sunset hour of 4:59

            when I pushed and strained
forth a child   of his immediate gaze

and suckle   of stinging milk-breast urge   its taste
            of my blackberry blood

of that first Brooklyn day outside after
            many child-feverish days   of racing

            down the exhilarating alleyway
into the spangled street   of sweating in the City of

            Fountains (of drinking at one   dipping
my feet in another)   of each ecstatic

swim   when I once fell in   got snow up my nose
      of the first time I picked blackberries

in Ithaca and bit in   of lavender smell   of the last time
      I kissed his sleepy face   or held

      her grasp: Is *forgetting*
the soul dying   finally with the body?

O Blessed One
      may it never be so

Moon Lilies (5:30 p.m.)

Frac
    tured light

        lil
ies pet
  al

    before

the darkening book (forbear)

until moo
    n ransom

    green pine shad
          ow
cast on the water   *O*

is the soul a re
    flection of a shade?

(I've lost my way)

Two turtles close to the pond floor
    Sap
      ling spring

    Manatee sighted offshore!

(Is this the path to you?)

In the suffering hour »
                                  sky
                                        oozing blood
                                  orange
pages gone dark

        Sabbath will be starlit

(Help me find you in time)

Rowing I'll be
              reclining
              in the middle of

                              where no one can re
                                                  mind me
                              of my name: (*M other*)

(and only you may find me)

83

Moth over City at Dusk

I am kneeling on spindly legs
   loris-ringed eyes in my wings » drawn toward
    this fading June bright » I cry out
    to you after having borne my son:
   Am I left to molder in the late light X-raying
the leaves of me?   I can no longer bear a child

And the city catacombs me as I listen to the laughter
     of women with babies » Honeycombs of light
     are taking him from me: surely with his dark glasses
he holds his own gaze » This is the hour of failed hope:

I am not sitting by the waters of Babylon
    my lyre is not yet unstrung » I am weeping
     into the watery age I have become » whatever beauty
    a turned page » Who praises the silk moth against
   translucent flowers » Zion streaking through the blinds
of memory » my sky is round as my scalloped life

O give me the strength to unbend my spine so I ascend
over the Hudson to that island of wet wool and kerchiefs
   where so many before us disembarked
     O do not teach me to number my days but to raise
     them up to you: in the roseate dusk over
   darkening waters » teach me to praise the impending
slivered light

Scroll and Pencil in Late Light

In the unspooling scroll
    how lilies look under
    water » what your hand
    holds in the sky » what sunfish
feel like in the skin of swim

in the flank of a wink
    of the iridescent sand eel » and zooplankton
    upon which whales feed
    when the cicada buzz » bullfrog
banjo thwang » subside   before

the darkling cricket ratchet » insect click:
    Let me give thanks to you for this peace
    the trees have ceased their murmurs
    the pond opens its aqua gown » a curtain
inside parts » memory of the unfurling scroll:

a baleen for catching holy letters
    of your name (*Yud-Hay-Vahv-Hay*)
    and sieving the salty debris out to sea
    For the still hour prevails
in the unscrolling spool

Globed and Curtained (7 p.m.)

        room of floor-to-ceiling sienna
each morning ring
the pulley to part the world

        ring it again to curtain off each night
this globed sky
upstaged by sycamore sighs »   bullfrog shore

        Great Pond does not sleep   it holds
the moon » rippling wind » all that I hope » points
of light   the heavens unveil   late in the midnight

        ink of surrender   This is the time when Pharoah broke
and we fled   with our bowls of unleavened dough »   our goats »
our lives   This the hour of pitched tents

        hour of finally settling in
to where I have been » time of full faith in the return
of manna   when my son at last sleeps inside

        his own I-will-have-been
If we have always been wanderers » most ourselves
in the desert   how then by this water

        this damp dark   do you bestow me
with your presence » nearer than at day-stark
when all your roses are black angels

        that tell me   even I must die

And the world isn't coming to an end

Thorny Bridge

                        into night
                clouds tearing across
        stars' oracle
                at summer's end
                        to recline blanket-down
                                        beachward
                        (waves »   black fracas)
                        to see the heavens
continually creating
                (Milky Way suckling our night-souls)
                        Over us spread your canopy of peace
                        your nine-o'clock favor
when embers glow and thorn-
                twigs crackle   final praise
                        in bright extinguishment
                                May it be your will
                        soon my eyes   (close)   in sleep   (   )
                dreams »   none fearful »   disturb
demons   nor find   (me)
                                O Creator of all light
                        under wings »   restore
                in peace   (lie down)   let me
rekindle before dawn

Nesting Book (Bedtime)

Pond

egg   of light

tree-nest

dark within

empurpled   book of sky

moon glides over »

reading an opened page

spiders come out to spin

bullfrogs'   song-dominion

Remember (us among) your creatures

we who hum (your blessings)

even in dreams

in our rain-

dropped slumber

Let your sky-cover hover over us

lest we sleep (our book closed)

For who else but the living can laud and read

all the hues you deck

the world with: warbler's yellow

breast »   bottle-blue sea »

iridescent-green dragon-

fly »   diamond-dropped

spider's web »   red-webbed lids

(my sleeping son's)

Arabesques of smoke

once blew » thr » ough » my   » eye

O Unpronounceable One

        May I still see

                in the violet hour

       Be with me

            in this   every sleeping

    waking

        hour   I call out   to you

Notes

"Manual for Living": The titles and inspiration for this sequence are from the Stoic philosopher Epictetus, culled from his *Enchiridion* and *Discourses*, as interpreted and reformulated by Sharon Lebell in *A Manual for Living* (New York: HarperOne, 1994).

"Black Paintings" were written in dialogue with Goya's *Black Paintings*, a series of paintings that may have been completed by him at the end of his life and are now housed in the Museo del Prado in Madrid.

"Of Hours" is a contemporary book of hours. These poems were initially inspired by a collection of paintings by Ellen Wiener titled *An Album of Hours* (several of which may be found at http://ellenwiener.com/paintings/) and by summers spent in Wellfleet.

The epigraph is from Rainer Maria Rilke's *Poems from the Book of Hours* (1941; New York: New Directions, 2009), translated by Babette Deutsch.

Acknowledgments

With gratitude to the following publications where these poems first appeared, sometimes in earlier drafts:

American Literary Review: "Psalm of the Flying Shell (4:30 a.m.)," "Lament of Shovel and Bell"; *Barrow Street*: Work in Progress Feature: "Recognize Mere Appearances for What They Are," "Everything Happens for a Good Reason," "No One Can Hurt You," Happiness Can Only Be Found Within," "Don't Demand That Things Happen as You Wish"; "Rose/Boat (8 a.m.)," "Moon Lilies (5:30 p.m.)"; *Connotation Press: An Online Artifact*: "Frail Pair," "Or, Judith," "Saturn," "Maja," "Moth Over City at Dusk"; *Cortland Review* (online): "Blue Ladder (9 a.m.)"; *Electronic Poetry Review* (online): "Blue Window (10 a.m.)," "Scissored In (3 p.m.)"; *Georgia Review*: "Always Act Well the Part That Is Given You"; *Green Mountains Review*: "Duel with Clubs," "Globed and Curtained (7 p.m.)"; *InPosse* (online): "Psalm of Morning Mist," "Duet of Tree House and Rain"; *Jewish Journal of Greater L.A.*: "Let Me Thrum (6 a.m.)"; *jubilat*: "Make Full Use of What Happens to You," "Morse and Fractals (Dawn Blessings)"; *Laurel Review*: "Thorny Bridge"; *Mead Magazine* (online): "The Reading"; *Nextbook* (online): "Let Me Thrum (6 a.m.)," "Thistle and Hull (7 a.m.)," "Scroll and Pencil in Late Light," "Nesting Book (Bedtime)"; *Ocean State Review*: "Atropos or the Three Fates"; *Omniverse* (online): "Desire Demands Its Own Attachment," "All Advantages Have a Price"; *Phati'tude Literary Magazine*, special issue, "Ekphrasis: A Conversation between Poets and Artists": "Pilgrimage"; *Poetry*: "Approach Life as If It Were a Banquet," "Everything Has Two Handles," "Our Duties Are in Relation to One Another"; *Poetry Northwest*: "Briefly Accept Events as They Occur," "Pay No Attention to Things That Don't

Concern You"; *POOL* (online): "Know What You Can Control and What You Can't," "Stick with Your Own Business," "Care for What You Happen to Have—There Is Nothing to Lose"; *RealPoetik* (online): "With Roses (6:30 a.m.)," "Green Laddered Thanksgiving (11 a.m.)," "Blackberry City and Sun Dial Talk (4pm): *Time*"; *Saint Ann's Review*: "Urn and Hooks (1 p.m.)"; *Salamander*: "Faithful Is Not Blind Belief," "Your Will Is Always," "Depth Lure Notebook"; *Spillway*: "Just This," "Never Regret"; *Spoon River Poetry Review*: "Events Themselves Are Impersonal and Indifferent"; *Talisman*: "Living Wisdom Is More Important Than Knowing About It," "The Coven," "The Dog," "The Fountain," "Two Old Folks Eating."

"Avoid Adapting Other People's Negative Views" appeared on *Poem-of-the-Day* (Academy of American Poets website).

"Window with Wild Garlic in Wellfleet" won third place in the 2008–2009 Anna Davidson Rosenberg Awards for Poems on the Jewish Experience.

"Let Me Thrum (6 a.m.)" appeared in *The Poets' Quest for God*, edited by Oliver Brennan, Todd Swift, and Dominic Bury (London, England: Eyewear Publishing Ltd., 2015).

With gratitude to the following institutions, where some of these poems were first drafted or revised: the Corporation of Yaddo, the MacDowell Colony, the Virginia Center for the Creative Arts, and Fundación Valparaiso.

Thank you to my friends and fellow poets for their support, particularly, Barbara Addleman, Jeanne Marie Beaumont, Barbara Blatner, Evan and Freda Eisenberg, Jody Feld, Jeff Friedman, Ellen Geist, Patti Horvath, Barbara Jaffe, Barbara Leeds, Phillis Levin, Ilene Levinson, and Alfredo Rossi. Especial gratitude to my stalwart editor, Ed Ochester. Finally, *todah rabah* to the Romemu community for giving me a new home.